Splashtastic
Rainy Day Activities
by

Activity 1	Save It for a Rainy Day	2
Activity 2	Rain, Rain, Go Away	4
Activity 3	A Downpour of Art Ideas	6
Activity 4	Cooking Up a Storm	8
Activity 5	Camping In!	10
Activity 6	It's Raining Cats and Dogs	12
Activity 7	Curl Up with a Good Book	14
Activity 8	The Write Stuff for a Rainy Day	16
Activity 9	Singing in the Rain	18
Activity 10	Name that Rainy Day Tune!	20
Activity 11	A Rainy Day Shower	22
Activity 12	Out in the Rain	24
Activity 13	Rainy Day Science	26
Activity 14	Cloud Bursts!	28
Activity 15	Thunderbolts	30
Activity 16	Somewhere over the Rainbow	32
Activity 17	Blowing in the Wind	34
Activity 18	A Chance of Showers	37
Activity 19	Under Construction	38
Activity 20	Got Game?	40
Activity 21	Puzzlers	42
Activity 22	Weather Word Search	43
Activity 23	Crossword Puzzles	44
Activity 24	Tangram Puzzlers	46

Editorial: Kristy Kugler, Christopher Kugler, Paul Rawlins
Art and Design: Andy Carlson, Robyn Funk, Magen Mitchell, Amanda Sorensen

ISBN 1-59441-723-7

Save It for a Rainy Day

Don't let rainy days get you down. Instead, think of them as special times to do projects you don't do on other days.

Rain Box

Keep a box of things to use on a rainy day. Put in some crossword puzzles, word searches, or a magazine you haven't read. Keep some special stationary and pens in the box to write letters to friends and family.

Putting on the Ritz

Nothing's more fun on a rainy day than dress up. Find some outdated clothes, gaudy jewelry, crazy hats, makeup, and props and have some fun! Invite friends over and have a party or a fashion show. Don't forget the camera.

Save It for a Rainy Day

Rainy Day To-Do's

Keep a list of things to do on a rainy day. Write your list down in a notebook or journal. You could clean out a closet or a drawer, put photographs in an album, or organize your CDs or DVDs. Or, you could write down things you've been meaning to do. Is there a puzzle you want to put together? What about making a collage out of pictures of your friends? How about baking cookies? Any time the clouds move in, pull your notebook out. You'll never have to worry about being bored again!

Top Ten List

When you're really bored, try this surefire boredom buster. Make your own Top Ten Lists. Here are some ideas: Top Ten Favorite Movies, Top Ten Favorite Songs, Top Ten Favorite People, etc. When you're done, put the list away. The next time it rains, take out your list and see if anything has changed!

Activity

1

Rain, Rain, Go Away

Sometimes it seems like the rain will never stop! On days like that, read through this pool of activities, and soon the rain will be gone.

Just Remember...

Whether the weather be hot,
or whether the weather is not,
we'll weather the weather,
whatever the weather
whether we like it or not!

Rain Gauge

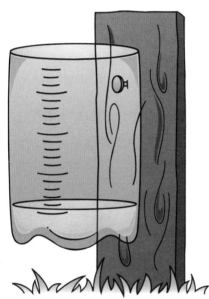

Perhaps it just seems like it has rained a foot! Find out for sure with a homemade rain gauge. Any container will work, but a clear 2-liter bottle with the top cut off is best. You can mark inches on the side with a magic marker. Then set your gauge outside and measure how much water comes down.

You may want to nail your rain gauge to a board so that it doesn't blow over during the storm. Be sure to seal any leaks where the nail went in.

Paper Chain

Another way to record the number of rainy days throughout the year is to make a paper chain. Add a chain link for each day it rains.

To make a paper chain, cut paper into strips between one and two inches wide. Thread the strip through the last link of the chain. Then staple or glue the ends together to make a new link.

Rain, Rain, Go Away

Rainy Day Weather Chart

If you start to feel like the rain will never end, cheer yourself up by making a weather chart to record the weather. Decorate your chart. Every day, draw a picture to represent the weather for that day. More than likely, there will be some sunny days to break up the rainy weather.

You Think You Have It Bad...

Mount Waialeale on the island of Kauai, Hawaii, averages about 460 inches of rain each year. That's over one inch of rain a day!

Activity

2

A Downpour of Art Ideas

What better way to pass the hours on a rainy day than to bring out the craft supplies and let the creative you come out.

Saving for a Rainy Day

Keep a box full of art supplies that you bring out only on rainy days. Fill the box with crayons, markers, tape, glue, and scissors. Add scraps from other projects or things from around the house to spark your imagination when the weather keeps you inside.

Splatter & Splash!

For an awesome rain design, squeeze a few drops of food coloring on a piece of paper. Then set the paper outside in the rain. Watch closely! The harder it is raining, the sooner your creation will be done.

Adult Help

Stained Glass Raindrops

Here is a great way to recycle old crayons for a rainy day creation. Peel any remaining paper off your old and broken crayons. Use an old cheese grater to grate the crayons. (Make sure this is OK before you start because you won't be able to use the grater on cheese again.) Put the crayon shavings on a piece of wax paper. Place another piece of wax paper over the shavings. Then ask an adult to heat up an iron and press the wax paper together until the crayon shavings melt. Don't press too long, or you'll have a black mess.

Peel the top layer of wax paper off the crayons. The melted crayons look like a stained glass window! Finally, take two pieces of blue construction paper and trace a raindrop shape onto one of them. Lay that piece on top of the other and cut out the raindrop outline. Cut carefully around the outline. What you want to end up with is the hole shaped like a raindrop, not the raindrop you drew. Glue the melted crayons between the two pieces of construction paper so the melted crayons show through the hole. Make several of these and hang them in your window. It adds color to a gray day.

Rainy Day Craft Recipes

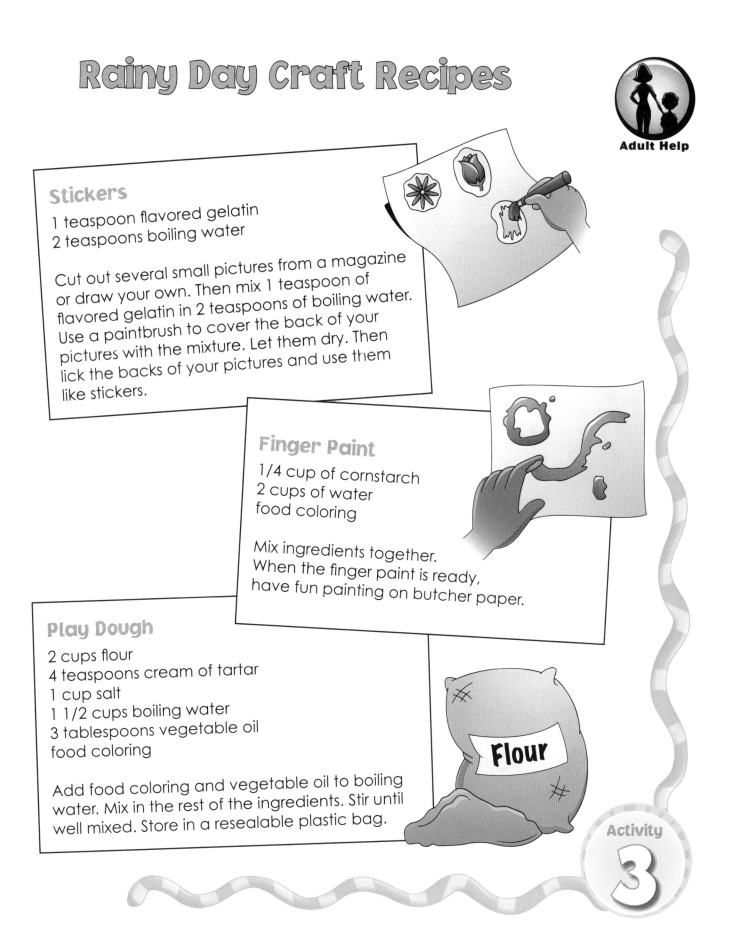

Adult Help

Stickers

1 teaspoon flavored gelatin
2 teaspoons boiling water

Cut out several small pictures from a magazine or draw your own. Then mix 1 teaspoon of flavored gelatin in 2 teaspoons of boiling water. Use a paintbrush to cover the back of your pictures with the mixture. Let them dry. Then lick the backs of your pictures and use them like stickers.

Finger Paint

1/4 cup of cornstarch
2 cups of water
food coloring

Mix ingredients together.
When the finger paint is ready,
have fun painting on butcher paper.

Play Dough

2 cups flour
4 teaspoons cream of tartar
1 cup salt
1 1/2 cups boiling water
3 tablespoons vegetable oil
food coloring

Add food coloring and vegetable oil to boiling water. Mix in the rest of the ingredients. Stir until well mixed. Store in a resealable plastic bag.

Flour

Activity
3

Cooking Up a Storm!

When a storm's brewing outside, create your own delicious storm in the kitchen. Nothing warms a house better than tasty treats fresh from the oven.

Mind Your Manners

Host a tea party or a luncheon. Practice using your best manners. Remember words like "please" and "thank you." Read up on other rules of etiquette.

Adult Help

Weave a Placemat

You will need two different large pieces of colored construction paper for each placemat. Cut slits in one of the pieces of construction paper as shown. Then cut the other piece into strips. Weave the strips in and out of the slits. Tape the ends.

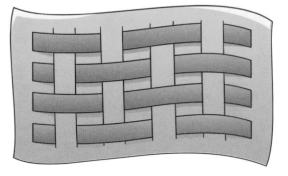

Cooking Up a Storm!

Adult Help

Hot Chocolate

6 tablespoons unsweetened cocoa powder
6 tablespoons sugar
salt
2 1/2 cups milk
2 1/2 cups light cream
1/2 teaspoon vanilla
cinnamon

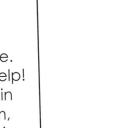

No rainy day would be complete without a cup of hot chocolate. Try this recipe for a special treat. Remember to ask an adult to help! Mix the unsweetened cocoa powder, sugar, and a pinch of salt in a sauce pan. Add the milk. Heat to dissolve. Add the light cream, the vanilla, and a pinch of cinnamon. Heat to barely boiling, stirring constantly. Pour into a mug and enjoy!

Mini Pizzas

pizza sauce
English muffin
mozzarella cheese, grated

Spread pizza sauce over an English muffin. Sprinkle with grated mozzarella cheese. Ask an adult to place your pizzas in an oven heated to 350 degrees for 10 minutes or until cheese melts.

Pretzels

bread dough
1 egg
1 tablespoon water
coarse salt

Buy some frozen bread dough at the grocery store or make your own. Roll a piece of dough into a "snake" about 10 inches long. Make a traditional curly pretzel or create letters or other shapes. Stir the egg and water together. Brush the egg mixture on your pretzel dough. Then sprinkle with coarse salt. Place on a cookie sheet and bake at 350 degrees until golden brown.

Activity

4

5

Camping In!

Rain may put a damper on camping out, but it is perfect weather for camping in.

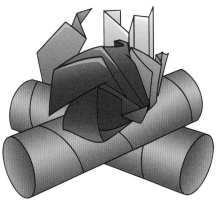

Setting Up Camp

Here's a campfire that will make even Smokey the Bear feel safe. Use some real firewood or some paper towel tubes. Crumple orange and yellow cellophane or tissue paper and place it between the logs.

Once you get the fire started, build a tent with blankets or sheets draped across the furniture. Bring out the sleeping bags, pillows, and flashlights to create a cozy rainy day hideaway.

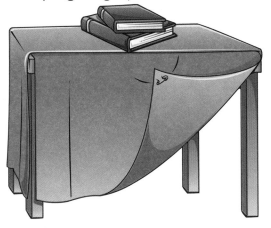

Can I Have S'more?

Make s'mores indoors! To make this tasty treat, sandwich a piece of chocolate and a marshmallow between two graham crackers. Place on a microwave safe dish and put in the microwave for 30 seconds. Enjoy!

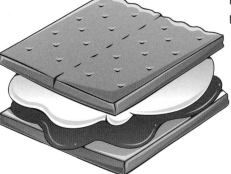

Adult Help

Camping In!

Hand Shadows

Get creative with hand shadows. Have someone go outside the tent with a flashlight. Shine the flashlight toward the wall of the tent. Put the flashlight on a chair so that you can have both hands free. Then make shadow puppet shapes with your hands. Some ideas are included below. Can you come up with some of your own?

Activity

5

It's Raining Cats and Dogs

Did you ever wonder where that saying came from? Well, no one's quite sure where the saying came from, but it means that it's raining very hard. Next time it rains, explore some of the weather words and phrases in our language.

Stranger Than Fiction

It has never rained cats and dogs, but on July 12, 1875, frogs fell from the sky during a rainstorm in Kansas City, Missouri! Scientists think that the frogs were swept up in the clouds by a tornado. And as the saying goes, what goes up must come down. Do some research about weird weather. Then write a story about some incredible weather.

Weather Words

Weather affects almost everything around us, even our language! Read these sayings that use weather words. Try to find out what they mean. Then use them in your speech and writing.

head in the clouds

cloud over his head

sunny disposition

clouds with silver linings

thunderous applause

quick as lightning

under the weather

Weather Riddles

Read these riddles and share them with your friends.
Then make up some weather riddles of your own.

What do you call it when it rains chickens?

Fowl weather

Why don't mother kangaroos like rainy days?

The kids have to play inside.

Why couldn't the meteorologist give the weather forecast?

He was under the weather.

What is the difference between a hurricane and a lion with a thorn in its paw?

A hurricane pours with rain, but a lion roars with pain!

What did the mother warn when it was raining cats and dogs?

Be careful not to step on poodles!

Activity

6

Curl Up with a Good Book

Do you like to curl up with a good book on a rainy day? Well, if you love to read, here are some rainy day activities just for you.

Books on Tape

Rainy days are great for listening to books on tape. Go to your library and check out a couple that you haven't heard yet. Or create your own. Use a tape recorder to record yourself reading out loud from your favorite book. Give the tape to a grandparent or other elderly friend to listen to on the next rainy day, or give it to a younger friend who can't read on his or her own quite yet.

Author, Author

Who is your favorite author? Do you like Barbara Parks? Is your favorite Beverly Cleary or Roald Dahl? Go to the library and check out every book you can by your favorite author. Compare the books. Which is your favorite and why? Write a letter to the author telling him or her why you like the books.

Rainy Day Reading List

The Cat in the Hat by Dr. Suess

Cloudy with a Chance of Meatballs by Judi Barrett

Thunder Cake by Patricia Polacco

A Drop of Water by Walter Wick

Come On, Rain by Karen Hesse

The Rain by Michael Laser

Rainy Day Stories and Poems edited by Caroline F. Bauer

Rainy Day Scavenger Hunt

Gather a stack of books, magazines, and newspapers. Heat up some hot chocolate (see recipe on page 9) and a treat or two. Snuggle up by the fire or cuddle up with a friend under a blanket. See who can find the most of the following items in a set amount of time. If there are more than two of you, you can work together in teams.

Find the following in a book or magazine.

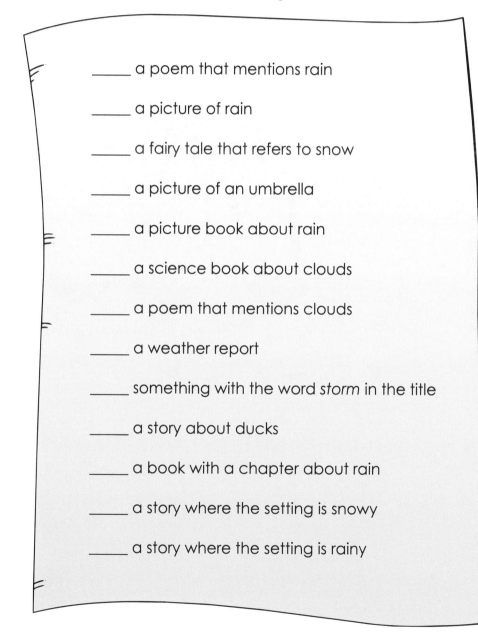

_____ a poem that mentions rain

_____ a picture of rain

_____ a fairy tale that refers to snow

_____ a picture of an umbrella

_____ a picture book about rain

_____ a science book about clouds

_____ a poem that mentions clouds

_____ a weather report

_____ something with the word *storm* in the title

_____ a story about ducks

_____ a book with a chapter about rain

_____ a story where the setting is snowy

_____ a story where the setting is rainy

Activity

7

The Write Stuff for a Rainy Day

There's no reason to be bored on a rainy day.
Just sharpen your pencil or click on your computer and experience
the 3 R's—Reading, 'Riting, and Rain!

Writing Box

Create a special writing box to hold all your special writing tools.
Fill the box with pencils, pens, crayons, markers, and colored pencils.
Add different types of paper, plus stickers and stencils.
Decorate the box.

ABC Book

Do you know a toddler or
two? Use the next rainy day
to create an alphabet book
just for them. Choose a theme
that your readers will like, such
as dinosaurs, bugs, or desserts.
Then think of things that
begin with each letter of the
alphabet. Draw pictures to go
with each letter.

Nursery Rhymes with a Twist

Write down as many nursery rhymes as you can remember. You might
need to get out a Mother Goose book to refresh your memory. Then
rewrite the rhymes with a new twist. See if you can update them.

Peter, Peter, hamburger eater

Put sugar on his fries to make them sweeter.

He ate until his belly swelled,

Then said, "I don't feel very well."

The Write Stuff for a Rainy Day

Choose a rain word and write an **acrostic** poem.
Acrostic poems spell a word if you read them from top to bottom.
Some acrostic poems use the letters from the word they spell to
start each line. Other acrostic poems spell the word in the
middle of the poem. The words in the poem are usually about the
word that is spelled out, too. See the examples below.

Radiant

Arc across the sky

Indigo and other colors

Never the same

Beautiful sight

Overlapping

Water miracle

Cotton candy in the sky

Lingers overhead

Opening for a downpour

Up so high

Dark and gray

Sun peeking through

Creates **T** errifying noises

Teams up with lig **H** tning

Take cover **U** ntil it stops

Sometimes far a **N** d sometimes near

Just wait it out. **D** on't be afraid.

Rumbl **E** s across the sky

Happens during a **R** ainstorm

Activity

8

Singing in the Rain

There is nothing like a song to chase away that gray, rainy day feeling.

Make your Own Music

Line up several drinking glasses or glass jars. Fill them with different amounts of water. Strike the outside or rim of the glass with a pencil. What do you hear? Which glass makes the highest sound? Which one makes the lowest sound? Try adding more or less water or using different sized containers to make beautiful music.

On the Net

http://www.niehs.nih.gov/kids/home.htm

Great site to visit on a rainy day to learn more about music.

It's Karaoke Time!

Gather your favorite CDs and a microphone and sing your heart out.

Singing in the Rain

Rain Sounds

Next time it rains, take time to listen to the rhythm of the raindrops. Recreate the sounds of rain inside your house. Start by gently rubbing two fingers together. Next, rub your hands together. Then tap on your legs. Finally, stomp your feet while you tap your legs. Reverse the order to make it sound as though the storm is letting up.

Make a Rain Stick

Tape one end of a paper towel tube closed. Fill the tube about halfway with rice or beans. Close up the other end with tape. Decorate your tube. Now you have a rain stick. Gently shake or tip your rain stick to create the sound of rain.

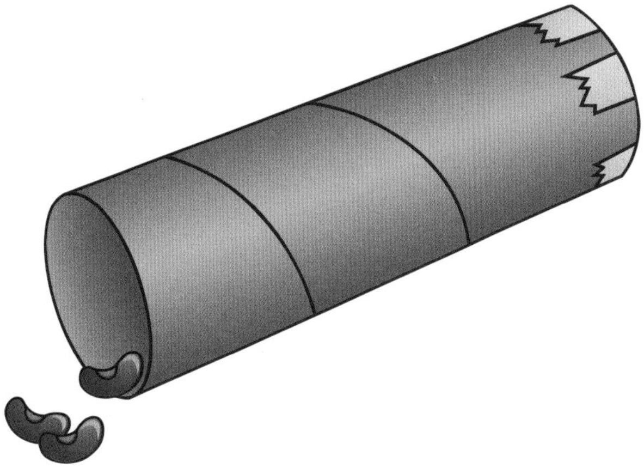

Weather Fact

Weather reports were published in newspapers in 1692.

Activity

9

Name That Rainy Day Tune!

Use the letters below each puzzle to figure out
these titles and phrases from rainy day songs.
(Note: the answers are at the bottom of page 21.)

1.

| S | O | M | E | W | H | E | R | E |

I A
R I R L U E R
S V M E W H H W D
S O E B N B E R E
O K A E S T O E E

2.

Y
O M N O A I
S O O E W A Y N
C A I E A A G A I R
R G M D A R T H E N

3.

I G
R T G I S
R N M A S I G
U I T N I I T
O O S A I N N N T S
P L D I O R S N G H E

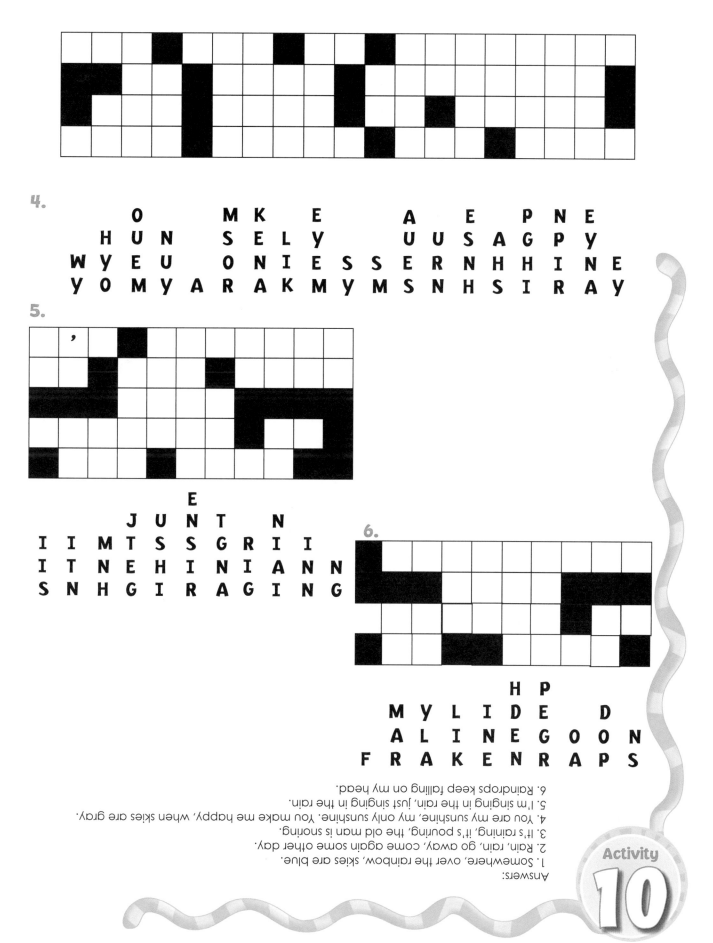

4.

O		M K	E		A	E	P N E
H U N	S E L Y		U U S A G P Y
W Y E U	O N I E S S E R N H H I N E
Y O M Y A R A K M Y M S N H S I R A Y

5.

```
        E
    J U N T   N
I I M T S S G R I I
I T N E H I N I A N N
S N H G I R A G I N G
```

6.

```
            H P
M Y L I D E     D
A L I N E G O O N
F R A K E N R A P S
```

Activity **10**

A Rainy Day Shower

You've heard of baby showers and wedding showers, but how about a rainy day shower? Break out the decorations, plan some games, and make some snacks! Before you know it, you've got a party to brighten even the darkest day.

Invitations

Cut a raindrop out of blue construction paper. Write *You're Invited to a Rainy Day Shower!* List the date, time, and place. Have your guests dress in rain gear. You could also have everybody bring a small gift to exchange. The gifts should have something to do with rainy weather.

You're invited to a Rainy Day Shower!

Shower Games

Mother Nature, May I?
To play Mother, May I? one person is "Mother." "Mother" stands at the finish line, and the other players stand at the starting line. "Mother" tells one player to do something such as "Take 2 baby steps" or "Take 4 giant steps." Before moving, the player must ask "Mother, May I?" Then Mother gives permission. If the player forgets, he or she is sent back to the starting line. The player who makes it to the finish line first becomes the next "Mother." Play "Mother Nature, May I?" the same way, except Mother Nature should give commands like, "*You may take five sprinkle steps*" or "*three thunder stomps*" or "*two lightning bolt leaps.*"

Umbrella Relay
Lay a closed umbrella on the floor. Players stand in lines on the other side of the room. Each player in turn runs to the umbrella, stands the umbrella up, puts his or her nose on the umbrella handle, and spins around the umbrella ten times. Then the player tries to run back to his or her line.

Shower Snacks

Rainy Day Drinks
Serve hot cocoa with marshmallows.
Serve punch with little umbrellas in the cups.

Raindrop Cookies
Bake sugar cookies in the shape of raindrops.
Decorate them with blue frosting and sprinkles.

Gift Exchange

If people bring gifts to your rainy day shower, try this fun game!
Seat the guests in a circle with one present in front of each guest.
Play a rainy day tune. When the music starts, the guests all pass the
presents to the right. When the music stops, so do the presents. Guests
stand up, holding the present they were holding when the music
stopped. Ask the guests to sit down by saying things like: "If you're
wearing red, please sit down." "If your hair is in a ponytail, please sit
down." Do this until only one person is standing up. That person may
open the gift, then leave the circle. Then the music starts again. Play
until everyone has opened a gift.

Shower Decorations

Decorate the room using
umbrellas, galoshes,
and rubber duckies.
Hang blue crepe paper
streamers straight down
from the ceiling. Don't
forget the clouds and a
rainbow!

Activity
11

Out in the Rain

No need to stay inside and sulk. Cut a hole in the bottom of a large garbage bag, and you have a brand new rain slicker!
Don't forget to splash in a few puddles.

A Rain Walk

Next time it rains, put on your rain slicker and boots and go outside and investigate. Take an adult along or ask for permission on where and how far to go. Look for signs of damage caused by the rain and how plants and animals react to the rain. Follow the rain in the gutter. Where does it go?

Float or Sink?

Take along a pocketful of twigs, pebbles, a coin, and some cork on your rainy day adventure. Try putting these things in a puddle. What sinks and what floats?

Adult Help

Canoe Come Out and Play?

Build this canoe and use it for boat races.

Fold a piece of cardboard in half.
Draw a side view of a canoe on one side of the
cardboard. Use the fold for the bottom of the
boat. Cut along the sides and top of the canoe.
Then use a needle and yarn to sew the curved ends, leaving the top
of the boat open. Cut some cardboard scraps to use as benches
inside your canoe. Decorate your boat, if you like.

To waterproof your canoe, ask your parents to put some wax in a
can; then set the can in a pan with a couple of inches of water and
heat until the wax melts. Have your parents use tongs to dip the
canoe in the wax. When the wax dries, you're ready to try out the
canoe! You may want to put some pebbles in the bottom to keep it
from flipping over.

Boats That Float

Get a ball of modeling clay. Drop it in a puddle outside. What
happens? Most likely it will sink. Now try to mold your clay into a
shape that will float. Find out how many marbles your clay boat can
hold. Try to make the smallest boat that holds the most marbles.

Boat Races

Float pieces of bark or homemade boats down the gutter during a
rainstorm. Have races against your friends and family.

Activity

12

Rainy Day Science

Take a few clouds and sprinkle them with a couple of raindrops, and what do you have? A science project!
Use the next rainy day to study the science of weather.

Create Rain

Make rain with steam and a dish of ice. Have an adult pour very hot water into a jar. Cover the jar with a plate. Put ice cubes on the plate and watch what happens. The cold plate causes the moisture from the hot water to form drops of water.

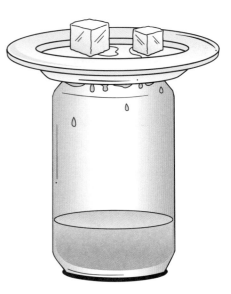

Rain Puzzle

Unscramble the letters below to make rain words. Use the letters in the circles to form a new rainy weather word.

N I R A

L E T S E

R O T S M

H D N U E T R

T I L H I G G N N

S E H S O R W

S I N R E P L K

L U C O S D

N U D P O R W O

L I H A

☐☐☐☐☐☐☐**B**☐☐☐☐☐

Measuring a Raindrop

Place a thin layer (1 to 2 inches) of flour in a flat pan. Take the flour pan outside just as a rainstorm is starting. Collect about 10 raindrops. Sift out the extra flour so just the little lumps that formed when the raindrops fell on the flour are left. Measure the size of the raindrops.

On the Net

Go to www.weatherwizkids.com for awesome information about rain!

Where Has the Water Gone?

Fill two glasses with the same amount of water. (Use glasses that are the same size.) Draw a line on the glass or use a piece of tape to mark the water level inside each glass. Put one glass in a warm place and the other glass in the refrigerator. Every day, check the water level in the glasses. After a few days, record your findings.

Activity
13

Cloud Burst!

Clouds are little messengers in the sky. Learning to read clouds can help you predict what kind of weather is coming.

Cloud Types

Learn about the different types of clouds and the weather they forecast.

Cumulus clouds are the big, fluffy, white clouds. They indicate fair weather.

Stratus clouds are low-lying gray clouds. They usually bring wet drizzly rain.

Cirrus clouds are high feathery clouds. The weather is fair, but a change may be on the way.

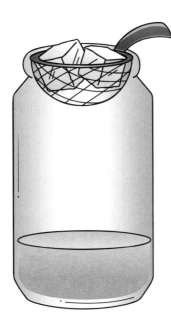

Make a Cloud

Pour a little warm water in a jar. Place a strainer filled with ice cubes in the mouth of the jar as shown. As the air in the jar cools, a cloud will begin to form.

Cloud Journal

Look up at the sky. Observe the clouds. Record your findings in a cloud journal. As you start to recognize what weather different clouds make, start making weather forecasts.

On the Net

Visit these websites for more information or activities on clouds.

www.cloudsrus.com

www.nasa.gov/audience/forkids/games

Paint Blot Clouds

Fold a blue piece of construction paper in half. Open the paper and pour a little white tempera paint on the center fold. Then refold the paper and press down to smear the paint. Open the paper again to see the unique cloud you have created.

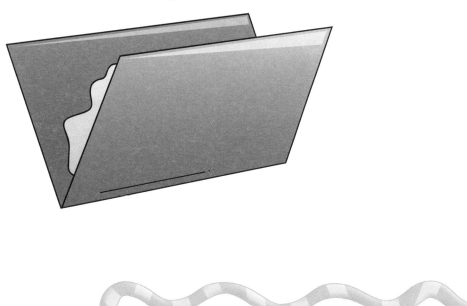

Activity
14

Thunderbolts

Where there is thunder, there is lightning, and vice versa.
Thunder and lightning bring excitement to any storm.
But beware: a lightning storm is very dangerous!

Facts about Thunder and Lightning

Lightning is about 54,000 degrees Fahrenheit. That is hotter than the surface of the sun!

More than 1,000 thunderstorms are happening around the world right now!

The diameter of an average lightning bolt is about 1" wide. The average length of a bolt is about 3 miles.

When lightning seems to flicker, you are seeing several bolts flashing at the same time.

Where's the Lightning?

If you hear one loud crack of thunder, the lightning is close by. If the thunder has a rumbling sound, it is further away.

Here's how to figure out how far away lightning is. Count the number of seconds between when you see the lightning and when you hear the thunder. Divide that number by 5. Your answer is the number of miles away the lightning is. If you do this a couple of times and find that the distance is getting shorter, the storm is headed your way. If the distance is longer, the storm is moving away from you. Any lightning within 6 miles can be dangerous.

Thunder Experiment

This experiment shows why thunder is so loud. Blow up a brown paper bag. Then pop it by clapping your hands together. Lightning heats up air, which makes the air expand (just like you made the bag expand). When air expands suddenly it creates a shockwave, and the ripples cause the noise we call thunder.

Safety in a Storm

Thunder may sound scary, but it is not dangerous. Lightning, however, is something to take seriously. Follow these rules to keep safe in a storm.

1. If you are inside during a lightning storm, stay inside. If you are outside, go inside or get in a car.

2. Avoid all metal (sheds, poles, bleachers, etc.), water, and trees. Metal and water attract electricity, and electricity will hit the tallest thing it can find first.

Activity
15

Somewhere over the Rainbow

For most people, rainbows mean hope.
Next time you are sulking over a rainy day, look for the rainbow!

Roy G. Biv

Have you ever heard of the famous Roy G. Biv? Actually, he isn't a real person. He's a way to remember the colors of a rainbow: <u>r</u>ed, <u>o</u>range, <u>y</u>ellow, <u>g</u>reen, <u>b</u>lue, <u>i</u>ndigo, and <u>v</u>iolet. Next time you see a rainbow, remember good old Roy G. Biv, and see if you can name the colors of the rainbow in order.

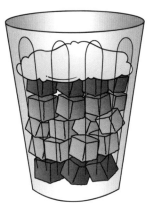

Rainbow in a Cup

Surprise your family and serve a rainbow in a cup for dessert. Make gelatin in several different rainbow colors. Once they have gelled, cut the gelatin into small cubes and layer the pieces in a clear glass or dessert cup. Top with whipped cream to represent the clouds.

Paper Rainbow

Use a pencil to draw a rainbow on a piece of white construction paper. Tear small pieces of colored construction paper. Glue the pieces on the rainbow in arcs in the order of Roy G. Biv. Overlap the pieces slightly as you move from one color to the next.

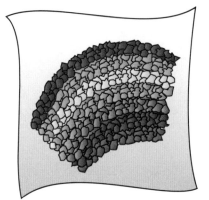

sunlight

raindrop

Rainbow Facts

Did you ever wonder if you could see a rainbow from the other side? Or how a rainbow gets in the sky to begin with? Well, the science of rainbows is really pretty simple. The sun must be shining from behind you with its rays reflecting on the water drops in the sky. When the rays hit the droplets, they refract (or bend) to form the arc and produce the colors we see.

I Can Make a Rainbow

For this experiment, you'll need to be in a dark room. Fill a glass with water. Tilt a piece of paper upward beside the glass of water as shown. Shine the flashlight through the water onto the paper. What do you see?

Activity

16

Blowing in the Wind

You can always count on the wind to stir things up on a rainy day. The wind can help you predict what kind of weather is coming your way. Wind from the north is cold, while wind from the south is warmer.

Make a Wind Sock

Pilots use wind socks to see which way the wind is blowing. You can make a simple (and colorful!) wind sock from a 9" x 3" piece of construction paper or poster board. Roll the paper strip into a ring and attach the ends together. Then tape different colors of crepe paper streamers to the paper ring. Attach a string and hang your windsock outside to watch the wind blow.

Wind Words

Unscramble these letters to find some wind words. Put the letters with numbers in the correct boxes to find out the name of a tool used to measure the wind.

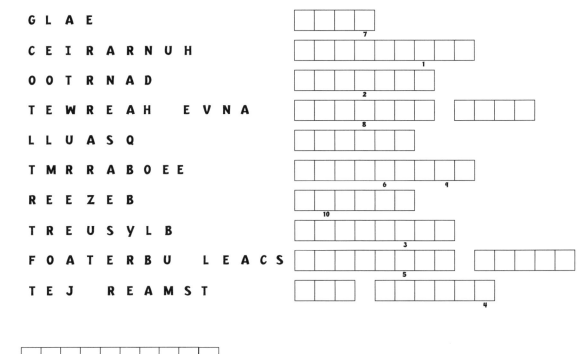

```
G L A E

C E I R A R N U H

O O T R N A D

T E W R E A H   E V N A

L L U A S Q

T M R R A B O E E

R E E Z E B

T R E U S Y L B

F O A T E R B U   L E A C S

T E J   R E A M S T
```

```
 1  2  3  4  5  6  7  8  9  10
```

Make a Pinwheel

Cut along the dotted lines below to make a pinwheel. Before you make the inside cuts, decorate your pinwheel with crayons or markers. Then make the cuts. Fold the corners marked X to the center of the paper. Push a pin through the middle of all four corners. Thread a small bead onto the pin on the back of the pinwheel. Push the pin firmly into the eraser of a new pencil. Take your pinwheel outside on a windy day and find out what direction the wind is coming from.

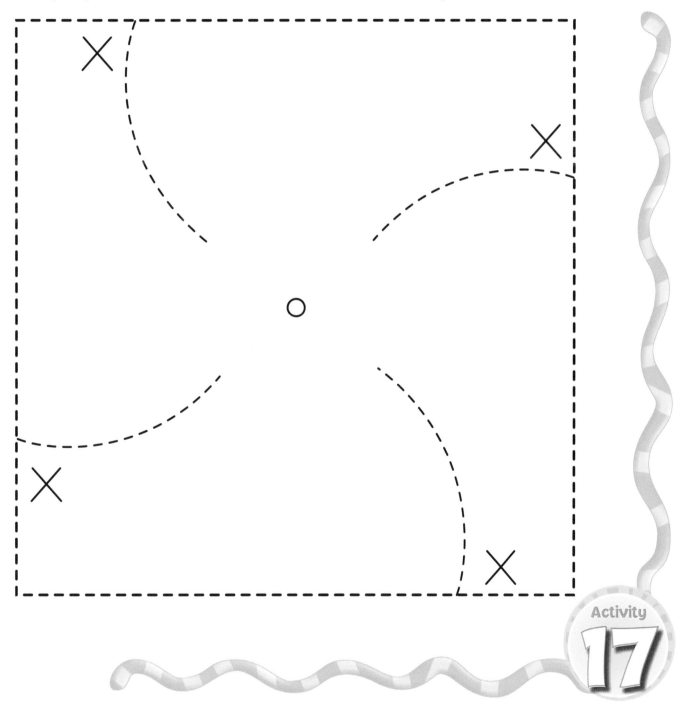

Activity
17

A Chance of Showers

Someone once said that weather forecasters are the only people paid well to be wrong! Try some of these ways of predicting the weather and see how well you do!

On the Air

Make your own predictions of the week's weather. Set up a news center with a map. Videotape your weather report. Tune in to your local news channel and watch how the pros do it. You might get some good ideas.

Reading a Weather Map

Look at the weather map below. Learn some of the weather symbols. Then when you watch the weather report you can amaze your family with your knowledge.

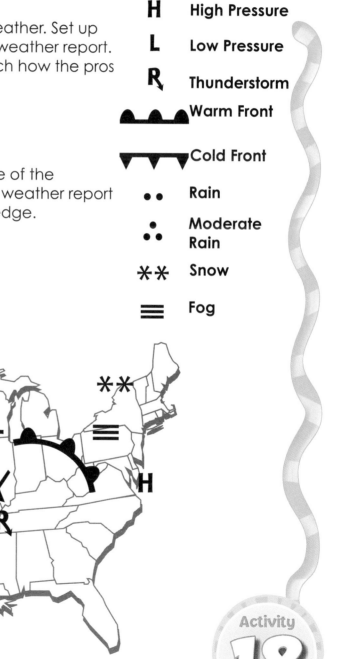

Activity 18

Under Construction

Rainy days are a great time to get out the building materials
and dust off your imagination.

Marble Maze

Use a shoebox lid to make this
fun maze game. Lightly sketch
a maze on the inside of the lid
with pencil. Then cut and glue
Popsicle or craft sticks onto the lid
to create the maze. Once you're
done, the challenge is to get a
marble from one end to the other
by gently rocking the box lid.

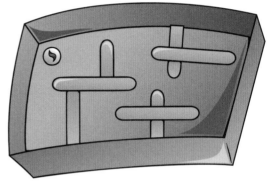

Spoolmobile

Here's a fun project. You'll need an empty spool, 2 matchsticks
with the heads cut off, a small washer, and a rubber band. Cut the
matchsticks so they are just a little shorter than the end of the spool is
wide. Thread the rubber band through the hole of the spool. Attach
it to the matchstick on the other side as shown (see A). On the other
side, thread the washer on before the matchstick (see B). Use the
matchstick on the side with the washer as the crank to wind the
rubber band until it is tight. Then set your Spoolmobile on a smooth
floor or table and let it go!

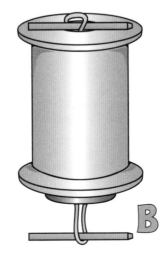

Box City

Ask your parents to save or gather
some boxes. The next time you are
stuck inside, build a city using the boxes. Paint windows, doors,
and signs on the buildings. Add as much detail as you want. If you
can get some large appliance boxes, you can even "live" in your
buildings!

An Obstacle Course

Build an obstacle course around your house. Ask your parents if it's
okay to move some furniture and use it for your obstacle course. Put
tape on the floor for balancing on, cardboard boxes for hurdles, a
blanket over a table for a tunnel. Crawl under coffee tables and over
chairs.

Activity

19

Activity

20

Got Game?

A rainy day is a perfect day to play games.
Pull out the games from the game closet or invent some of your own.
Then gather your family and friends and have a good time!

Balloon Bonanza

With a 99¢ bag of balloons, you can create your own mini Olympics.
Try some of these games.

Balloon Basketball

Blow up a balloon and set up two empty
trash cans at the opposite ends of the
room. Then play basketball. Dribbling
might be too hard, but you can pass
the balloon from person to person until
someone scores by putting the balloon
in their basket.

Javelin Throwing Contest

Use long, thin balloons. See who can throw the "javelin" the farthest.

Balloon Volleyball

Tie a string between two chairs to divide the room in half. The string
and chairs will serve as the net. Then divide the group into two teams.
Have each team take one side of the net. The object of the game
is to keep the balloon up in the air and get it over the net. (Try it with
the teams sitting down!)

Bottle Bowling

You need 10 empty plastic 2-liter bottles and a tennis
ball. Line the bottles up as shown. Stand about nine feet
away and roll the tennis ball toward the bottles. Remove
the bottles that were knocked over. Roll a second time
to see how many more bottles you can knock over. Give
yourself one point for every bottle knocked over in two
rolls. The person with the most points wins!

Got Game?

How Long Will It Take?

All you need for this game is a watch with a second hand. Time yourself to see how long it takes you to tie your shoes or run up and down the stairs. With your friend or sibling, brainstorm a list of things you can time yourself doing. Try to improve your time the next go around.

Clean Out the Game Closet

A rainy day is the perfect time to organize the game closet. Pull out each game and check for missing pieces. Take time to play a game or two as you go. Try to remember the last time you played each game.

The Great Mix-Up Game

Take the pieces from several games and make up your own game. For example, every time you pass Go on the Monopoly board, you pick up two letter tiles from the Scrabble game. Use the letter tiles to make a word. Receive $50 for each letter used.

Activity

20

Puzzlers

Don't let a little rain dampen your brainpower!
Try these puzzles to keep your brain sharp.

Make Your Own Puzzle

Cut a picture out of a
magazine. Glue it on a piece
of poster board. Then cut it
into pieces. Try to do the puzzle
yourself. Then see if your friends
and family can put together
your puzzle. Store the pieces in
an envelope

Work on a Puzzle

Brush the dust off one of the puzzles in the
back of the closet. Turn on an old movie
and make some popcorn for a snack. Go
easy on the butter, or you might create
quite a mess!

Weather Word Search

Find the weather words in this puzzle.
Words can be found up, down, across, diagonally, and backwards.

cirrus   **clouds**   **cumulus**
hail   **hurricane**   **lightning**
stratus   **rainbow**   **raindrop**
sleet   **thunder**   **nimbostratus**

b	n	l	t	u	v	a	w	s	b	r	u
p	i	x	h	t	h	a	i	l	t	a	c
o	m	y	s	s	h	s	j	u	e	i	l
r	b	g	e	u	g	u	y	c	e	n	o
d	o	n	r	n	t	n	n	l	l	b	u
n	s	i	n	f	a	a	c	d	s	o	d
i	t	n	y	v	n	c	r	f	e	w	s
a	r	t	e	b	v	b	i	t	w	r	c
r	a	h	l	n	h	z	m	r	s	v	w
x	t	g	f	a	l	i	t	s	r	q	b
y	u	i	o	s	u	r	r	i	c	u	k
m	s	l	c	u	m	u	l	u	s	r	h

Activity 22

Crossword Puzzle I

Across

1. pieces of ice that fall like rain
3. an arc of color in the sky
4. water that falls from clouds
6. a sudden, heavy rainfall
8. a sudden, heavy rain

Down

1. strong rain with strong winds
2. to rain gently
3. homophone of *rain*
5. frozen rain
7. rain happening

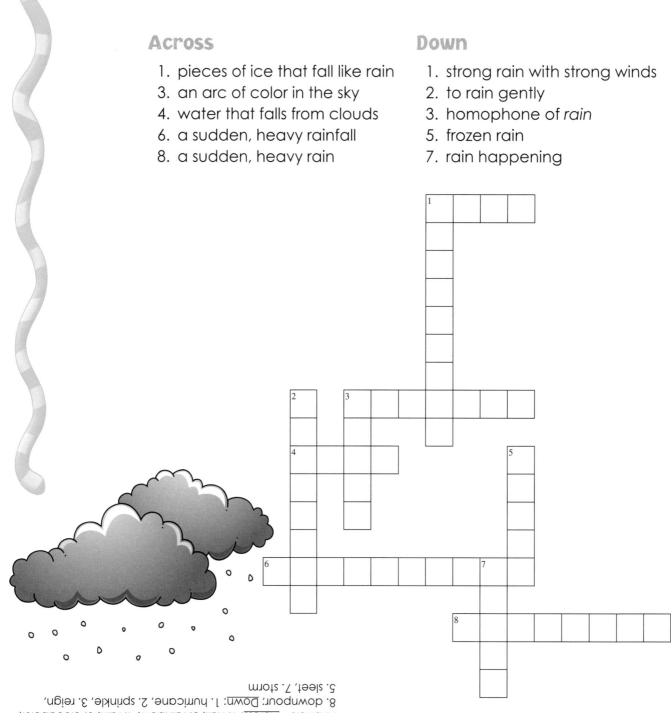

Answers—Across: 1. hail, 3. rainbow, 4. rain, 6. cloudburst,
8. downpour; Down: 1. hurricane, 2. sprinkle, 3. reign,
5. sleet, 7. storm

Crossword Puzzle II

Across

1. puffy white clouds
5. a severe winter storm
8. loud noise created by lightning
11. weather prediction
12. the amount of rain that falls

Down

2. a flash of light during a storm
3. high, feathery clouds
4. a very strong wind
6. light rain
7. an instrument used to measure wind
9. the pattern of weather in an area
10. low-lying gray clouds

Answers—Across: 1. cumulus, 5. blizzard, 8. thunder, 11. forecast, 12. rainfall; Down: 2. lightning, 3. cirrus, 4. gale, 6. drizzle, 7. anemometer, 9. climate, 10. stratus.

Activity
23

Tangram Puzzle

This ancient Chinese puzzle uses 7 simple pieces to make many different shapes and pictures. This puzzle has 5 triangles, 1 square, and 1 rhombus. Cut out the puzzle on page 47. Use the pieces to make some of the pictures below. Then create some of your own pictures and record them for others to solve.